F You, Box

STERLING
New York

An Imprint of Sterling Publishing
1166 Avenue of the Americas
New York, NY 10036

ISBN 978-1-4549-1719-9

Distributed in Canada by Sterling Publishing
℅ Canadian Manda Group, 664 Annette Street
Toronto, Ontario, Canada M6S 2C8
Distributed in the United Kingdom by GMC Distribution Services
Castle Place, 166 High Street, Lewes, East Sussex, England BN7 1XU
Distributed in Australia by Capricorn Link (Australia) Pty. Ltd.
P.O. Box 704, Windsor, NSW 2756, Australia

For information about custom editions, special sales, and premium and corporate purchases, please contact Sterling Special Sales at 800-805-5489 or specialsales@sterlingpublishing.com.

Manufactured in China

2 4 6 8 10 9 7 5 3 1

www.sterlingpublishing.com

F You, Box

(AnD other observations
OF My CAt's inner DiALogue)

by katie cook

STERLING
New York

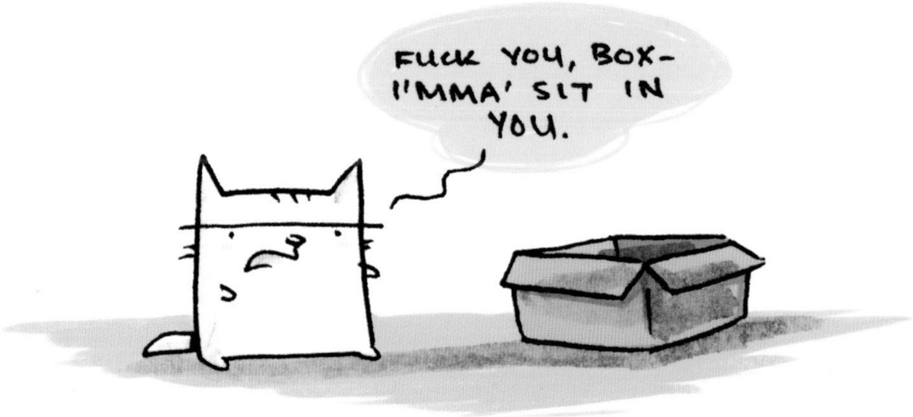
FUCK YOU, BOX-
I'MMA' SIT IN
YOU.

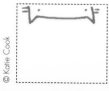

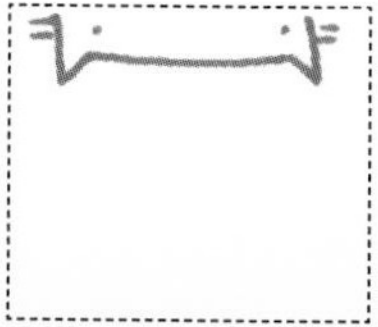

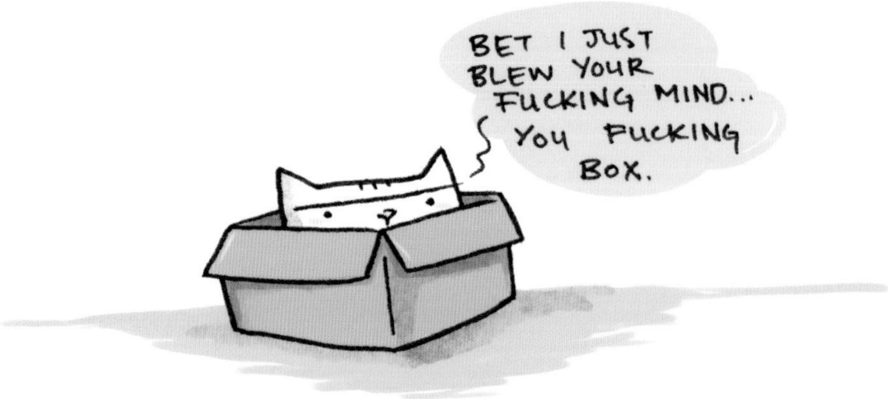
BET I JUST BLEW YOUR FUCKING MIND... YOU FUCKING BOX.

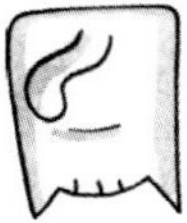

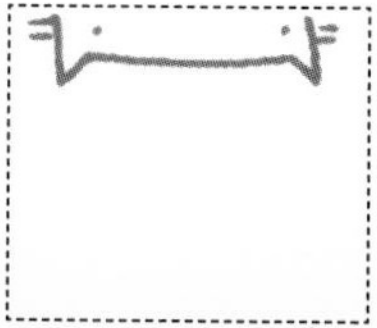

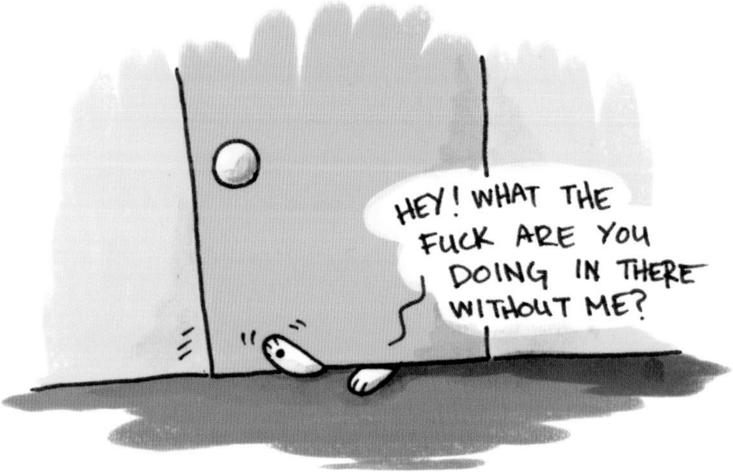
HEY! WHAT THE FUCK ARE YOU DOING IN THERE WITHOUT ME?

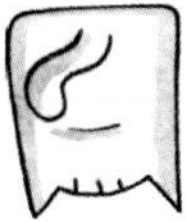

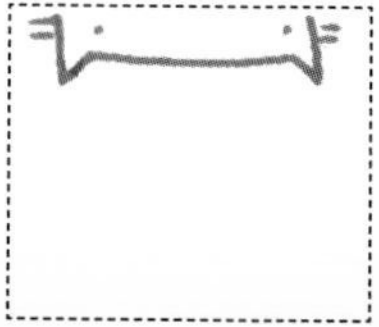

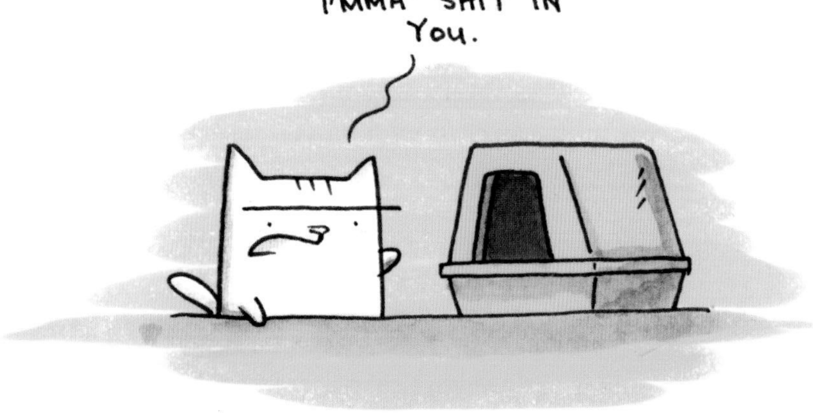
I'MMA' SHIT IN YOU.

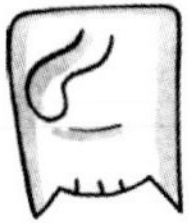

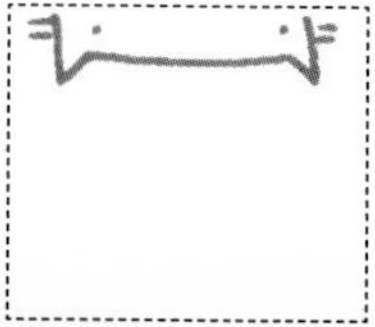

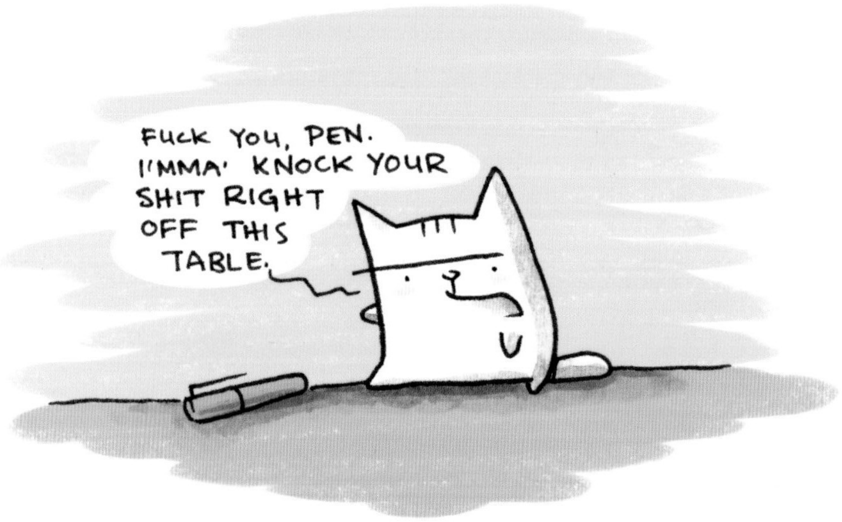
FUCK YOU, PEN. I'MMA' KNOCK YOUR SHIT RIGHT OFF THIS TABLE.

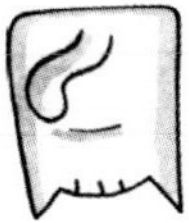

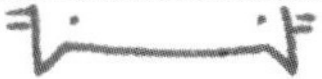

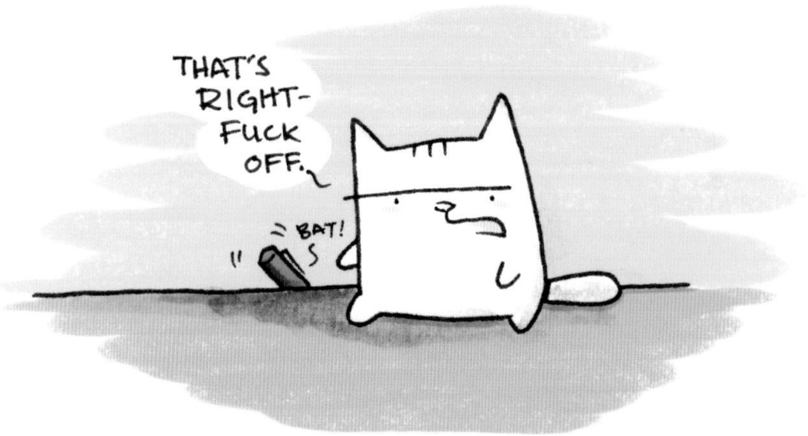
THAT'S RIGHT- FUCK OFF.
BAT!

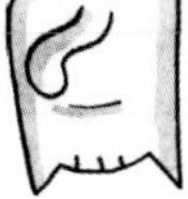

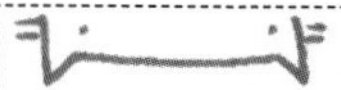

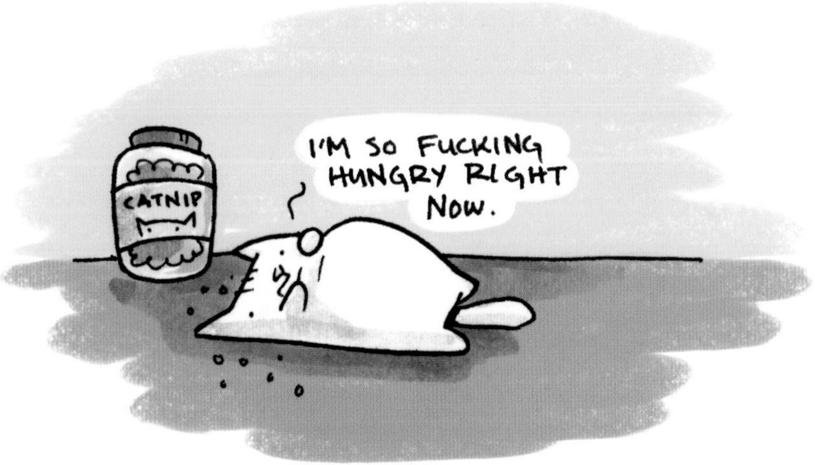
I'M SO FUCKING HUNGRY RIGHT NOW.
CATNIP

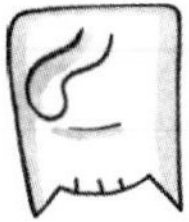

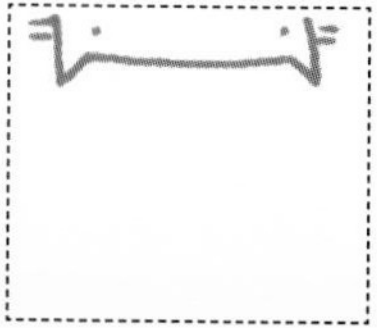

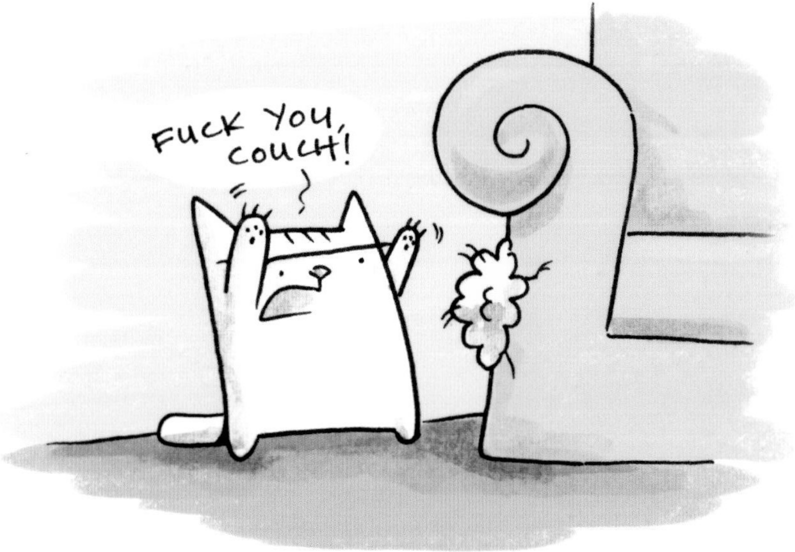
FUCK YOU, COUCH!

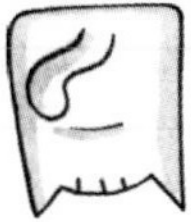

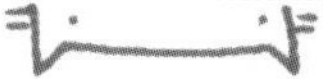

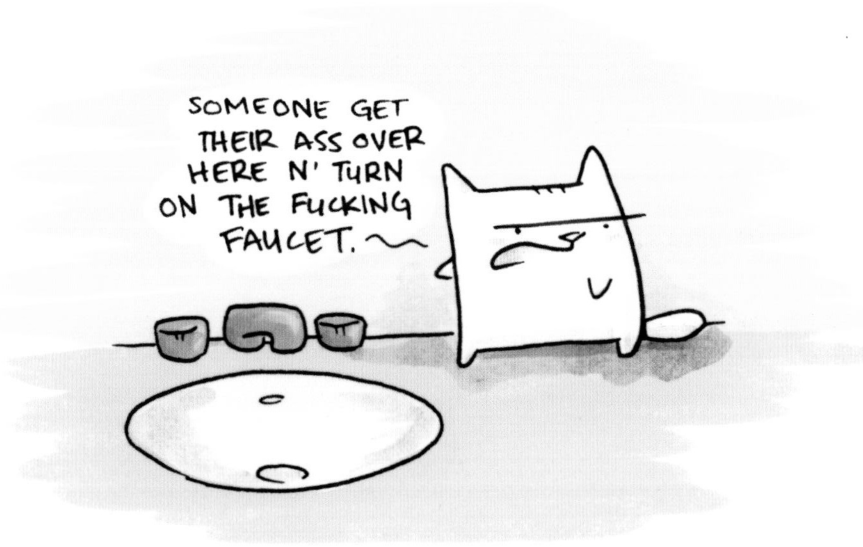
SOMEONE GET THEIR ASS OVER HERE N' TURN ON THE FUCKING FAUCET.

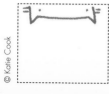

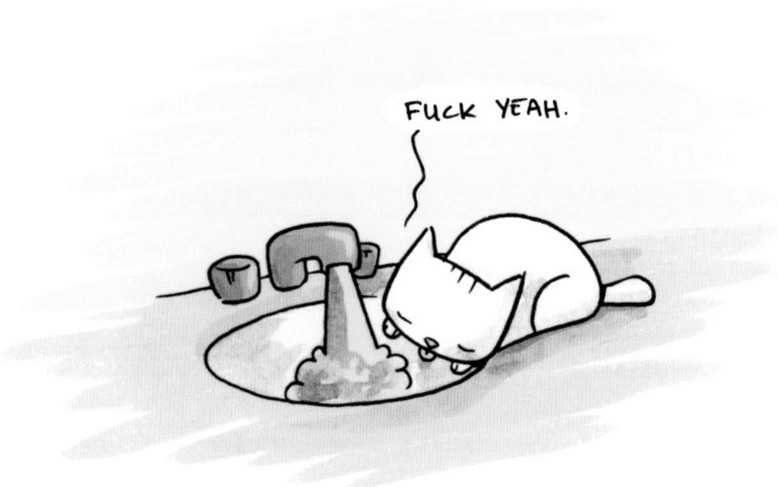
FUCK YEAH.

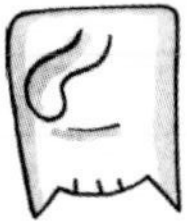

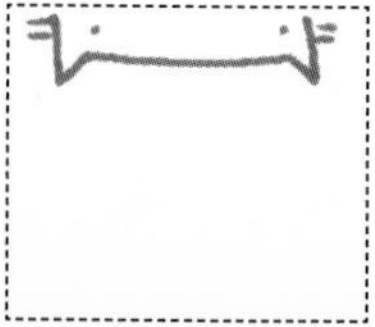

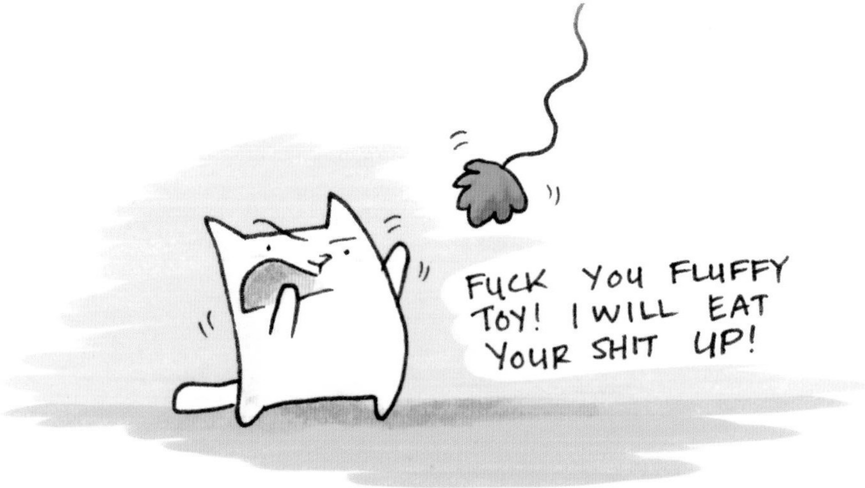
FUCK YOU FLUFFY TOY! I WILL EAT YOUR SHIT UP!

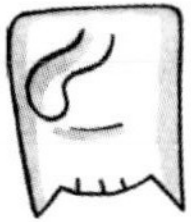

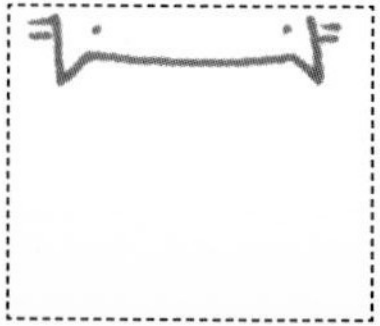

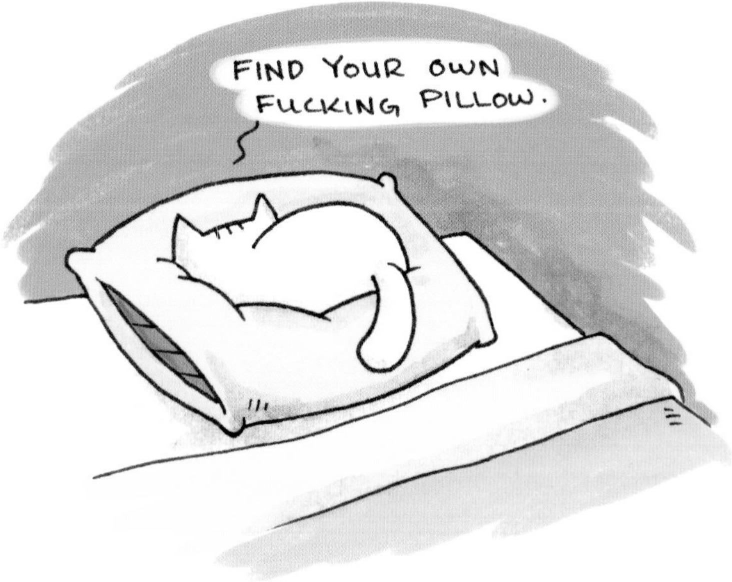
FIND YOUR OWN FUCKING PILLOW.

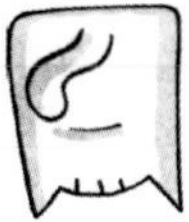

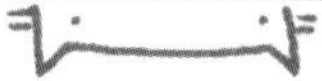

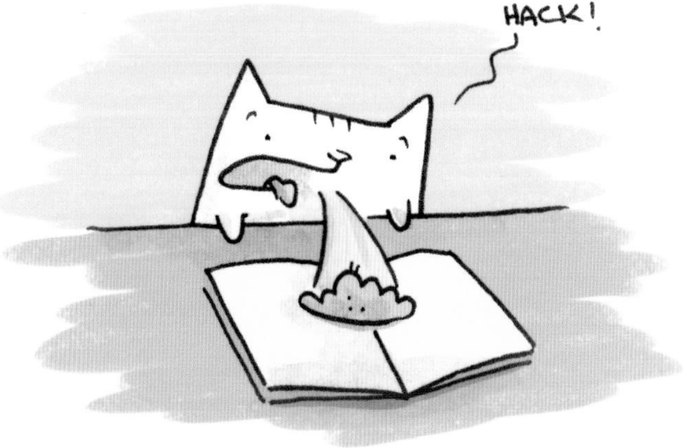
HACK!

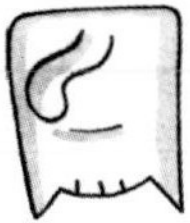

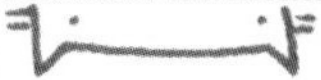

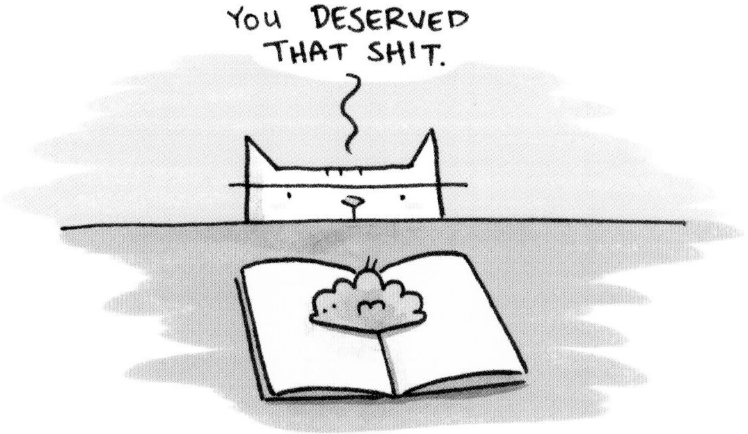
YOU DESERVED THAT SHIT.

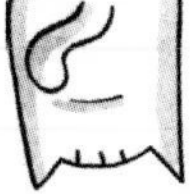

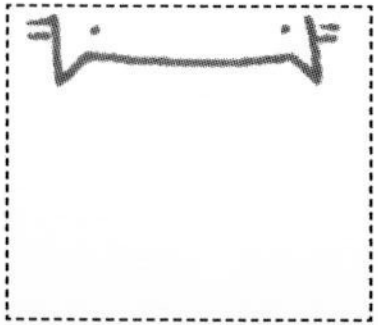

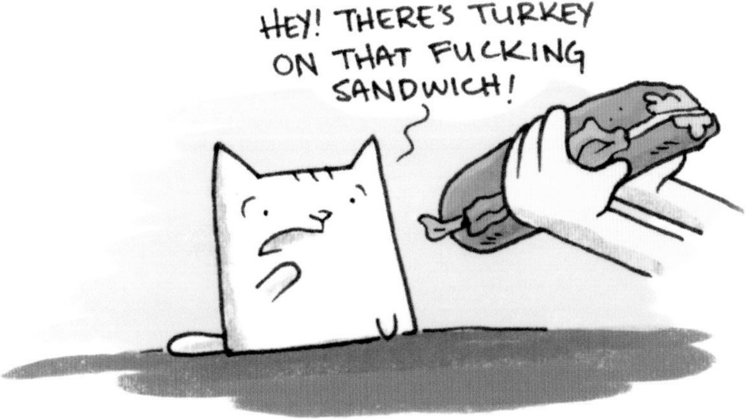
HEY! THERE'S TURKEY ON THAT FUCKING SANDWICH!

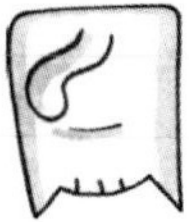

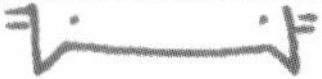

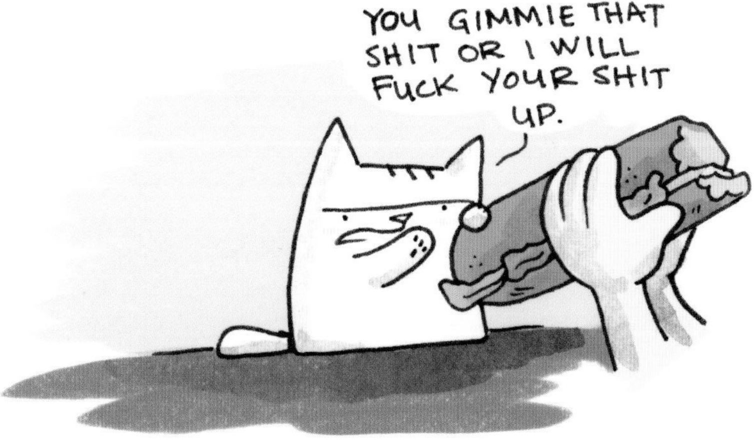
YOU GIMMIE THAT SHIT OR I WILL FUCK YOUR SHIT UP.

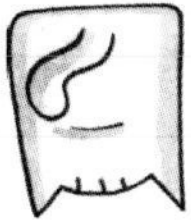

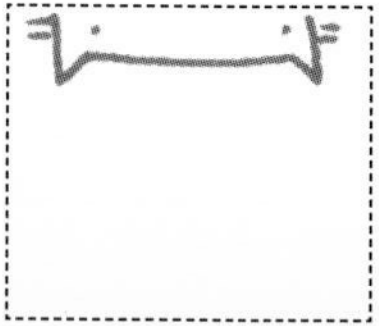

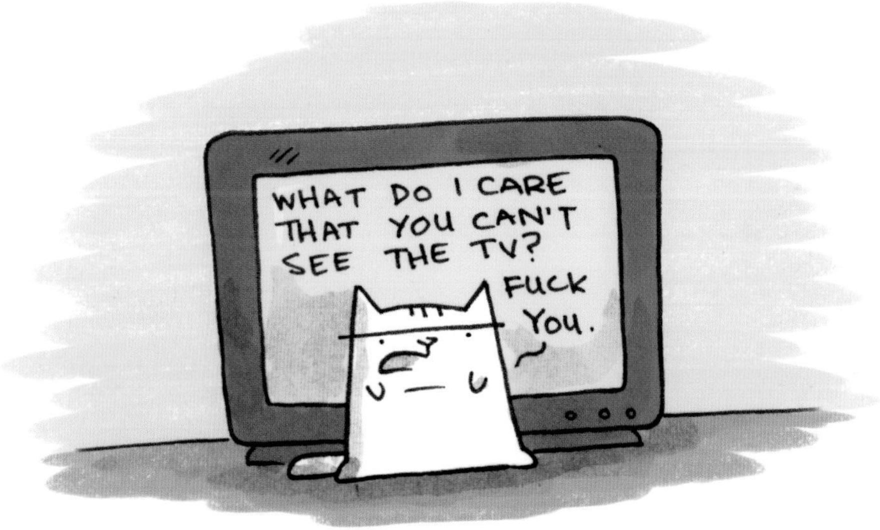
WHAT DO I CARE THAT YOU CAN'T SEE THE TV?
FUCK YOU.

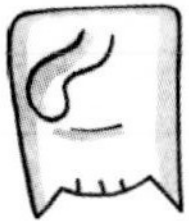

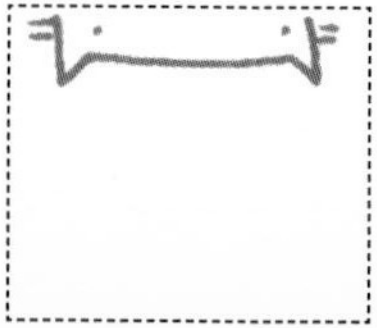

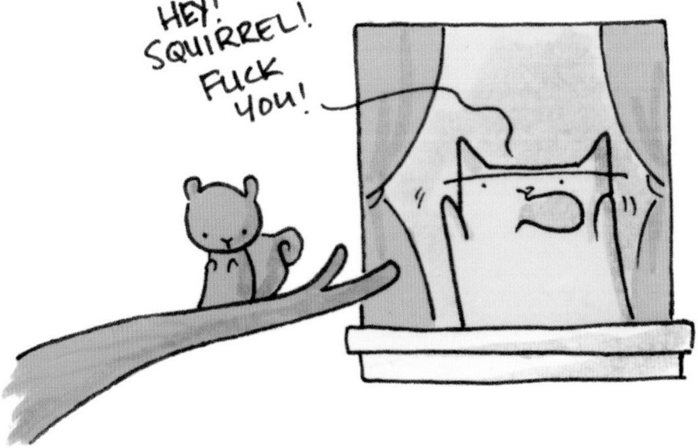
HEY! SQUIRREL! FUCK YOU!

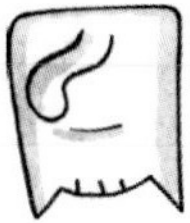

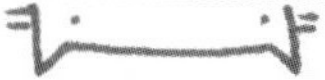

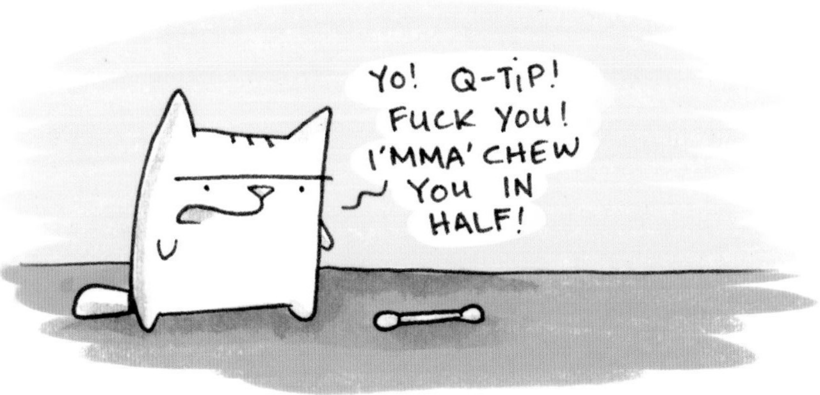
YO! Q-TIP! FUCK YOU! I'MMA' CHEW YOU IN HALF!

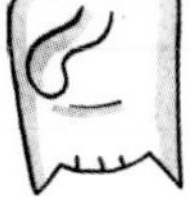

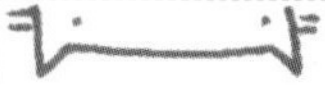

HEY ... BAG.
FUCK YOU. I'LL
FUCK YOUR
SHIT UP.

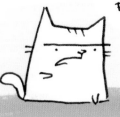

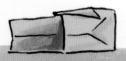

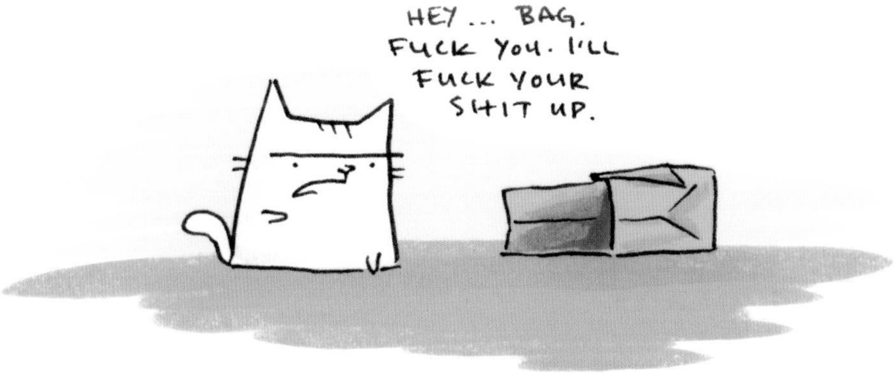

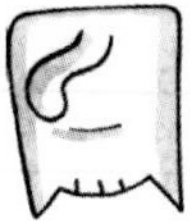

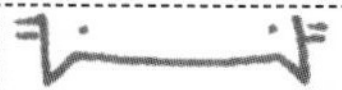

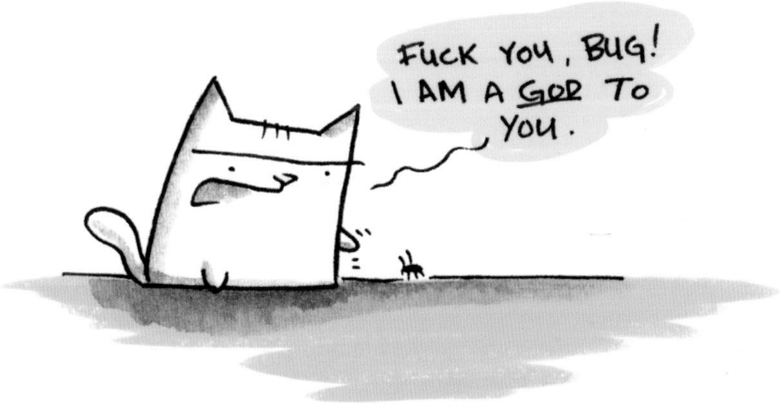
FUCK YOU, BUG!
I AM A GOD TO
YOU.

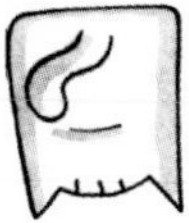

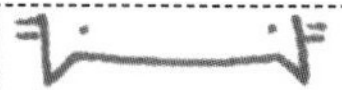

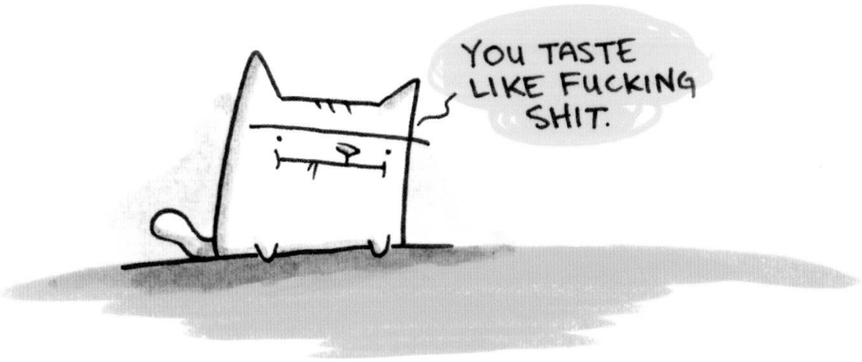
YOU TASTE LIKE FUCKING SHIT.

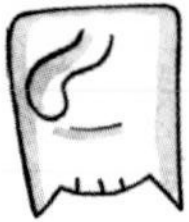

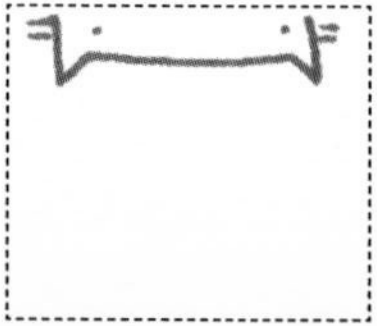

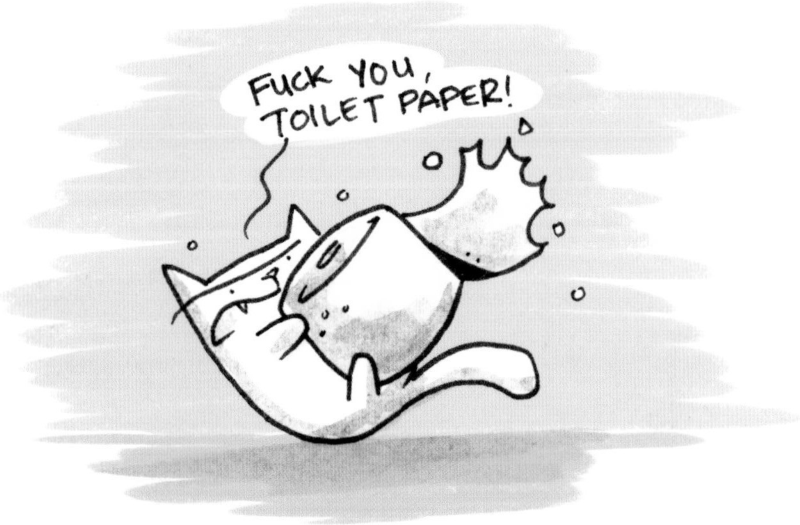
FUCK YOU, TOILET PAPER!

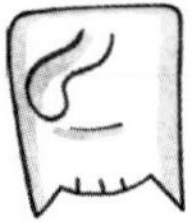

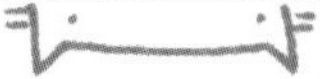

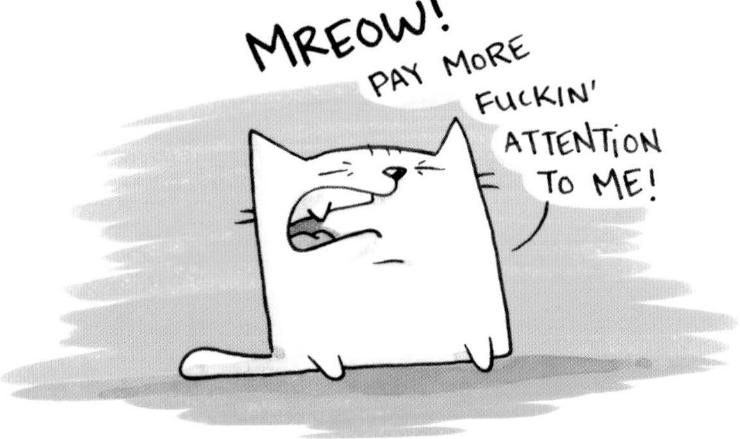
MREOW!
PAY MORE FUCKIN' ATTENTION TO ME!

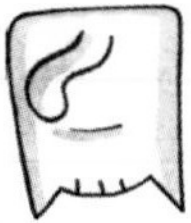

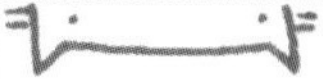

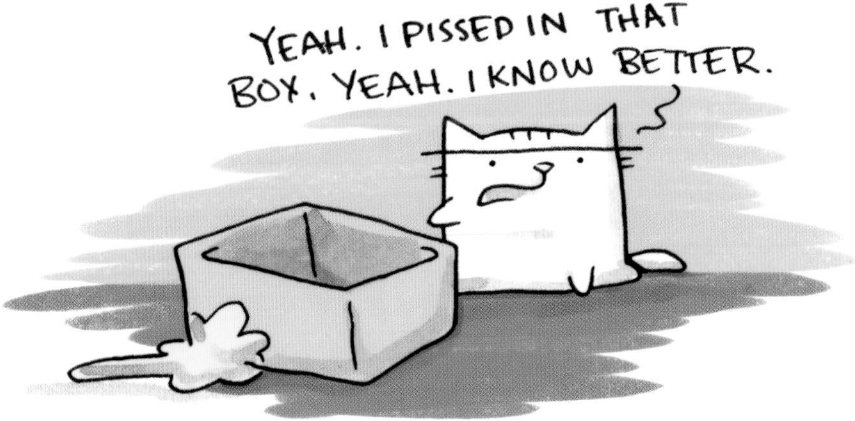
YEAH. I PISSED IN THAT BOX. YEAH. I KNOW BETTER.

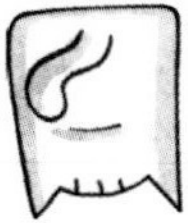

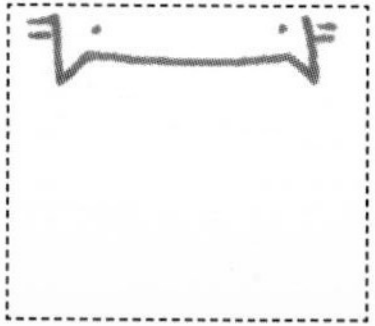

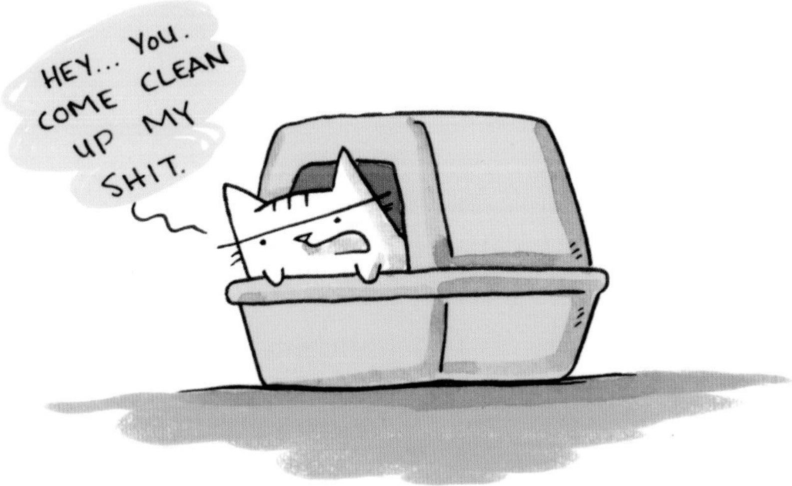
HEY... YOU. COME CLEAN UP MY SHIT.

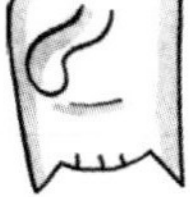

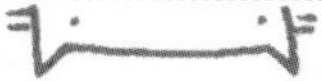

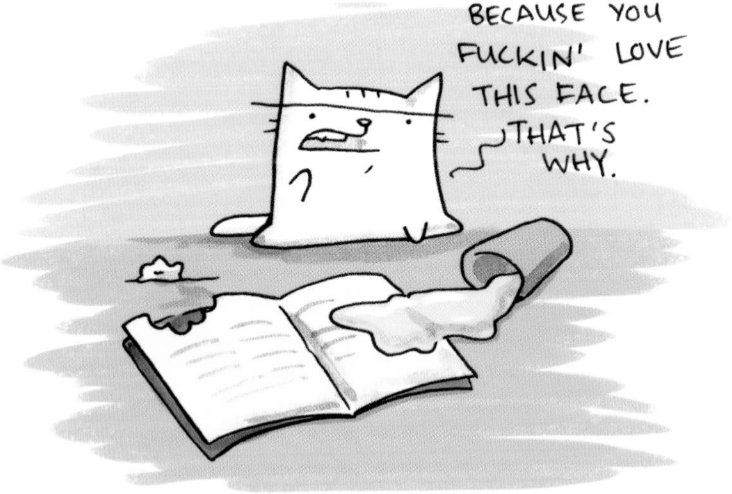
BECAUSE YOU FUCKIN' LOVE THIS FACE.
THAT'S WHY.

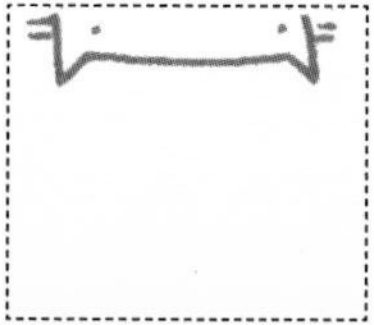

© Katie Cook

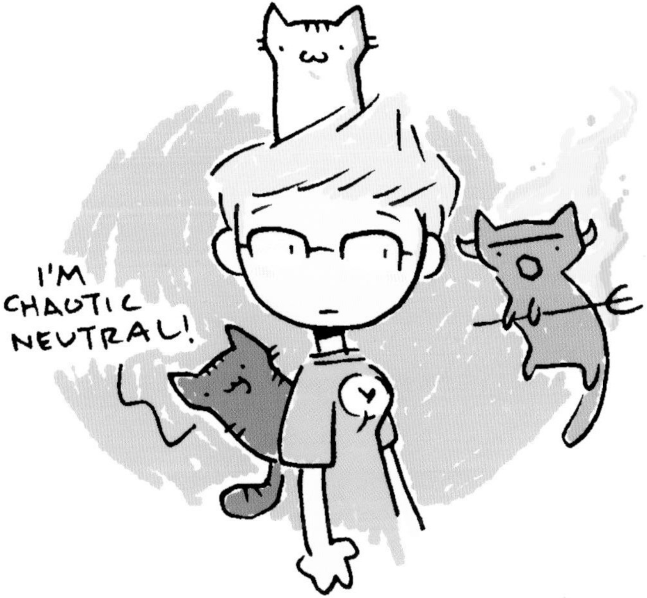
I'M CHAOTIC NEUTRAL!

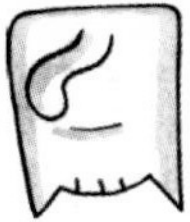

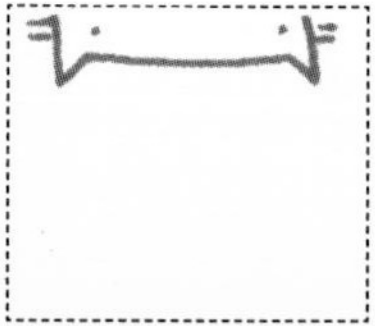